PISCES

HOROSCOPE

& ASTROLOGY

2025

Mystic Cat

Suite 41906, 3/2237 Gold Coast HWY

Mermaid Beach, Queensland, 4218

Australia

islandauthor@hotmail.com

Copyright © 2024 by Mystic Cat

Time set to Coordinated Universal Time Zone (UT±0)

All rights reserved. This book or any portion thereof may not be reproduced or used in any manner without the publisher's express written permission except for the use of brief quotations in a book review.

The information accessible from this book is for informational purposes only. None of the data should be regarded as a promise of benefits. It should not be considered a statutory warranty or a guarantee of results achievable.

Images are used under license from Fotosearch & Dreamstime.

Contents

January	16
February	24
March	32
April	40
May	48
June	56
July	64
August	72
September	80
October	88
November	96
December	104

Hello there,

Let me explain why my horoscope books may give different readings for each zodiac sign. The sky is always bustling with astrological activity, and I want to focus on what's most important for each star sign.

Every zodiac sign is unique, and the planets up above affect them differently. When I create horoscopes, I pay extra attention to the most critical astrological events for a specific sign. Some days, there might be lots of stuff happening in the stars, but one thing stands out as the essential factor for a particular zodiac sign.

I also consider which planet rules a sign and its associated element. This in-depth consideration helps me tailor my interpretations to match a sign's characteristics.

Ultimately, my goal is to provide you with unique advice and insights that match the cosmic influences for your sign. By focusing on what makes each sign special, I hope to help you understand yourself better and navigate the energies around you. Embracing your sign's strengths and challenges is the key to making my horoscopes feel uniquely aligned for you.

Cosmic Blessings,

Sia Sands

PISCES 2025
HOROSCOPE & ASTROLOGY

Four Weeks Per Month

Week 1 – Days 1 - 7

Week 2 – Days 8 - 14

Week 3 – Days 15 - 21

Week 4 – Days 22 – Month-end

PISCES

PISCES

Pisces Dates: February 19th to March 20th

Zodiac Symbol: Pair of Fish

Element: Water

Planets: Jupiter, Neptune

House: Twelfth

Color: Sea Green

Pisces is the twelfth astrological sign in the zodiac and falls under the Water element. People born under the Pisces sign are known for their compassionate, intuitive, and artistic nature. The symbol of Pisces, the fish swimming in opposite directions, represents duality, fluidity, and the connection between the conscious and unconscious mind.

Pisces individuals are characterized by their sensitivity, empathy, and deep emotional depth. They often have a strong intuition and are attuned to the emotions and needs of others. Ruled by Neptune, the planet of imagination and spirituality, Pisceans have a rich inner world and are drawn to creative and artistic pursuits.

Pisces is in the Twelfth House of the zodiac and is associated with introspection, spirituality, and hidden matters. This placement emphasizes Pisces' connection to life's mystical and spiritual aspects and their ability to tap into the collective unconscious.

Sea green is often associated with Pisces due to its connections with intuition, emotion, and tranquility. This color reflects the empathetic qualities of Pisces individuals.

In summary, Pisces embodies compassion, intuition, and artistic expression. Those born under this sign often have a deep connection to their emotions and a strong ability to understand the feelings of others. Their creativity and spiritual inclinations make them adept at connecting with others profoundly and emotionally.

The Chinese Zodiac is a system that assigns an animal sign to each year in a 12-year cycle, and each animal is associated with certain personality traits and characteristics.

The Year of the Snake, in particular, holds special significance within Chinese culture and is rich in symbolism.

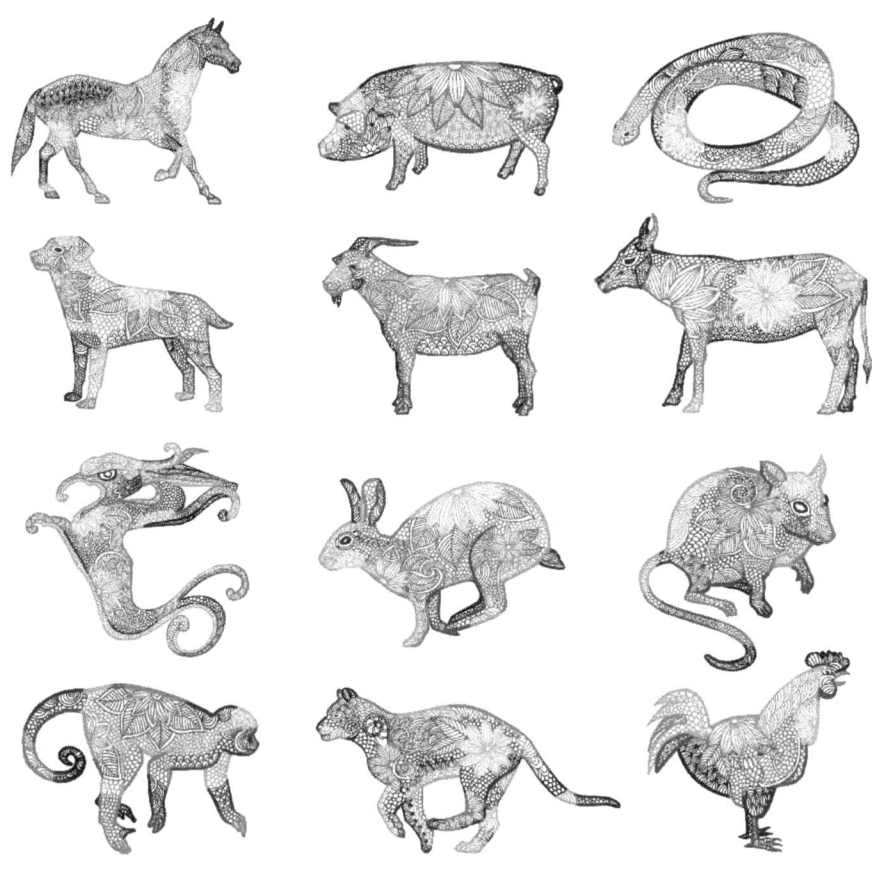

2025

The Chinese Year of the Snake

Pisceans are known for their empathy, creativity, and intuitive nature. They possess a deep connection to their emotions and often seek to explore the inner dimensions of life. When the Year of the Snake arrives, it introduces a unique blend of energies that can resonate with and challenge the Pisces personality.

During this year, Pisceans might find themselves drawn to the Snake's qualities of introspection and transformation. Just as snakes shed their skin to grow, Pisces individuals could shed emotional baggage or self-limiting beliefs, allowing personal growth and healing.

The Year of the Snake encourages Pisces to tap into their intuitive and imaginative capacities. It's a time for them to explore their artistic and spiritual pursuits, delving into the realms of creativity and inner wisdom, much like the Snake's ability to sense its environment with heightened perception.

Pisces' natural sensitivity aligns well with the Snake's adaptability. This year might inspire Pisceans to navigate the currents of life with greater flow and acceptance while remaining true to their empathetic nature.

In relationships, the Year of the Snake could encourage Pisceans to form connections on a more profound level. Just as snakes rely on their senses to understand their surroundings, Pisces individuals might seek to truly comprehend the emotions and motivations of those around them, fostering deeper bonds.

While Pisces are known for their dreaminess, the Year of the Snake invites them to explore their inner world even more deeply. It doesn't mean losing their imaginative spirit; instead, it's about combining their emotional depth with a deeper understanding of their desires and aspirations.

Ultimately, the Year of the Snake offers Pisces emotional healing and spiritual growth. By tapping into the Snake's symbolism of shedding the old and embracing the new, Pisceans can refine their intuitive gifts, foster deeper connections, and continue navigating life's waters with a blend of sensitivity and wisdom.

PISCES 2025
HOROSCOPE & ASTROLOGY

JANUARY WEEK ONE

🌙 With the Moon gracefully stepping into Capricorn, you'll experience a notable shift in your emotional landscape. Capricorn's energy brings discipline and ambition to the forefront of your emotions. It's akin to a cosmic CEO taking charge of your feelings, prompting you to set goals and get down to business. You'll become more focused on long-term plans and ambitions, prepared to tackle challenges with a determined spirit. Channel energy productively using the responsibility that Capricorn brings.

● New Moon: The universe is handing you a fresh canvas and a palette of possibilities. Whether you're eyeing a new job, embarking on a significant project, or seeking a fresh perspective on your professional life, this is your cosmic reset button. So, grasp your dreams and make a wish because the universe is listening and ready to support your journey to the stars.

🌘 As the Moon moves into Aquarius, anticipate a shift towards independence and innovation in your emotional realm. Aquarius' energy is akin to a cosmic rebel, encouraging you to embrace individuality.

JANUARY WEEK ONE

Brace yourself for a celestial embrace of romance and whimsy as Venus elegantly glides into the mystical waters of Pisces. In the realm of Pisces, love knows no bounds, and you're the dreamer navigating its boundless depths.

Buckle up and prepare for a cosmic collision as Mars stands toe-to-toe with Pluto. Harness this potent energy judiciously, directing it towards an unwavering pursuit of your loftiest goals.

The Moon's graceful entrance into Pisces paints your emotional landscape with dreamy, intuitive hues. Imagine a cosmic lullaby coaxing introspection and gently guiding your spirit to mystical realms.

When the radiant Sun extends a harmonious sextile to steadfast Saturn, it's akin to a cosmic nod of approval for your unwavering dedication and diligent efforts.

With the Moon's fiery entrance into Aries, a dynamic shift in your cosmic energy awaits. It's as though a spark of celestial electricity ignites your passions and invigorates your inner drive.

JANUARY WEEK TWO

As Mercury gracefully enters the earthy realm of Capricorn, your thoughts take on a more structured and pragmatic tone. It's like the universe hands you a sturdy planner and a set of goals to conquer. You'll find that patience and a systematic approach to communication serve you well during this cosmic alignment.

The Moon's entrance into communicative Gemini lights up your social circuits. Your curiosity gets a cosmic nudge, making this a prime time for engaging in lively conversations, networking, and gathering information. Your mental antenna is on high alert, ready to pick up fascinating tidbits from every corner of the universe. Use this intellectual energy to your advantage.

As the Moon gracefully glides into Cancer, your emotional landscape takes on a nurturing hue. You'll feel a profound connection to your roots and loved ones, craving cozy moments and emotional bonding.

When Mars forms a harmonious trine with Neptune, it's like a dose of cosmic magic infused into your actions. Your drive is guided by inspiration and intuition.

JANUARY WEEK TWO

⚡ The Sun's harmonious trine with Uranus ignites your inner innovator. You're open to new experiences, unconventional ideas, and exciting changes. It's a cosmic invitation to embrace personal growth, break free from routine, and explore uncharted territories.

The Full Moon casts its radiant glow, illuminating your achievements and goals. This lunar climax is a moment of culmination and realization. It's a time to celebrate your successes, acknowledge your progress, and, if necessary, recalibrate your direction. You stand under the cosmic spotlight, basking in your lunar glory.

As the Moon transitions into theatrical Leo, your desire for attention and self-expression takes center stage. Your inner performer is ready to dazzle the cosmic audience, and you'll be drawn to activities that allow you to showcase your unique talents and flair.

Venus square Jupiter adds a touch of indulgence and desire for pleasure. It's a cosmic reminder to savor the sweetness of life while maintaining balance during this cosmic interplay.

JANUARY WEEK THREE

◐ When the Sun opposes Mars, it's like a celestial tug-of-war between your ego and your actions. This energetic clash can fuel assertiveness but may also lead to conflicts. It's a reminder to find a healthy balance between your desires and how you pursue them.

☽ The Moon's ingress into meticulous Virgo encourages attention to detail and a desire for order. You'll find satisfaction in organizing your surroundings and focusing on practical tasks. It's a time when a well-structured to-do list becomes your best friend.

⚡ The Sun's harmonious sextile with Neptune infuses your life with enchantment and spiritual insight. Your intuition is heightened, and you'll find connecting with your inner dreams and creativity easier. It's a cosmic nudge to explore your artistic and mystical side.

💜 Venus's conjunction with Saturn brings a sense of responsibility and commitment to your relationships and values. While it may sometimes feel heavy, this cosmic alignment encourages you to take love and financial matters seriously, ensuring a solid foundation.

JANUARY WEEK THREE

As the Moon gracefully moves into Libra, your desire for balance and relationship harmony becomes prominent. You'll seek fairness and cooperation, making it an ideal time for resolving conflicts and enhancing your social connections.

Mercury's sextile with Saturn and Venus adds a touch of diplomacy to your communication style. You'll find it easier to express your thoughts with clarity and charm, making it an excellent period for negotiations and heartfelt conversations.

The Sun's transition into Aquarius marks a shift towards innovation and unconventional thinking. Your focus turns to community and social causes, and you'll embrace your individuality.

The Sun's conjunction with Pluto ushers a decisive period of transformation and rebirth. It's like a cosmic phoenix rising from the ashes, urging you to relinquish what no longer serves you and embrace your power.

As the Moon ventures into intense Scorpio, emotions run deep, and you'll seek profound connections. It's a time to delve into mysteries and explore your desires.

JANUARY WEEK FOUR

🚀 Mars sextile Uranus: This cosmic alignment brings energy and a desire for action. You'll feel excitement and a willingness to embrace change and innovation.

🗣 Mercury opposed Mars: When Mercury opposes Mars, it's a cosmic debate between your thoughts and actions.

💡 Mercury trine Uranus: This harmonious aspect sparks brilliant ideas and innovative thinking. Your mind is like a lightning bolt of inspiration, making it an excellent time to explore new concepts.

🌙 Moon ingress Sagittarius: As the Moon ventures into adventurous Sagittarius, your emotions crave exploration and expansion.

💝 Venus trine Mars: Love and passion harmoniously coexist during this celestial dance. Your romantic and sensual energies are in sync, making it an ideal time for intimate connections and creative endeavors.

🌙 Moon ingress Capricorn: Emotions take on a more serious tone as the Moon moves into pragmatic Capricorn. You'll be focused on your goals and responsibilities, prioritizing stability.

JANUARY WEEK FOUR

☾ Moon ingress Aquarius: Emotions take on an intellectual and humanitarian tone as the Moon moves into Aquarius. You'll prioritize your sense of community and individuality, seeking out like-minded individuals.

☿ Mercury conjunct Pluto: This intense cosmic meeting delves into the depths of your thoughts and communication. You'll uncover hidden truths and may be drawn to explore psychological or esoteric subjects.

● New Moon: The New Moon marks a fresh beginning and a chance to set intentions for the future. It's a cosmic reset button for your desires and aspirations.

◉ Uranus turns direct: As Uranus resumes its forward motion, you'll experience a shift towards greater freedom and innovation in your life. It's like a cosmic awakening, encouraging you to embrace your individuality and pursue your unique path.

⚡ Sun trine Jupiter: This harmonious aspect radiates positivity and abundance. It's a time of expansion and growth, where opportunities flow and optimism soars.

FEBRUARY WEEK ONE

♥ When Venus aligns in a tender embrace with Neptune, it's as though the universe orchestrates a love symphony just for you. Love and romance take on a dreamy and ethereal quality during this celestial dance. Your heart swells with compassion, and you may find yourself drawn to creative expressions of affection. This cosmic union encourages you to embrace your inner poet, allowing your feelings to flow through art, music, or heartfelt words.

💬 Mercury's harmonious trine with Jupiter is like a symphony of wisdom and eloquence in your mind. Your mental faculties are sharp, and your intellectual pursuits are graced with optimism and curiosity. Conversations flow effortlessly, and you'll find it easier to grasp expansive ideas and communicate them gracefully.

🌙 Once the Moon settles into sensual Taurus, you'll appreciate the stability and comfort of your surroundings, relishing in sensory experiences like good food, soothing music, and the beauty of nature. This lunar phase encourages you to ground yourself and indulge in self-care.

FEBRUARY WEEK ONE

🌶 Venus's ingress into fiery Aries brings a bold and adventurous spirit to your love life. You'll be unapologetically passionate in your affections, not hesitating to make the first move. This cosmic shift empowers you to express your desires with confidence.

⏩ Jupiter's direct motion signals a turning point for growth and progress. If specific plans or projects had been in a holding pattern, now is the time to move them forward with renewed enthusiasm. The cosmic winds are again at your back, propelling you toward your aspirations.

As the Moon transitions into communicative Gemini, your social and intellectual curiosity takes center stage. Your communication skills shine, and you'll relish the opportunity to connect. This lunar phase encourages networking, learning, and exploring perspectives.

💝 Venus's sextile with Pluto adds depth and intensity to your relationships and desires. It's as though your connections undergo a profound transformation, encouraging you to delve into the depths of your emotional bonds.

FEBRUARY WEEK TWO

☽ As the Moon gracefully makes its way into nurturing Cancer, your emotions become attuned to the comforts of home and family. This lunar shift encourages you to prioritize emotional connections and seek solace in familiar surroundings. Your sensitivity is heightened, making it an ideal time for heartfelt conversations and acts of care.

☉ The Sun's conjunction with Mercury marks a period of heightened mental activity and clear communication. Your thoughts and words align effortlessly, allowing you to express yourself with precision and confidence. It's when your ideas shine brightly, making it an excellent moment for meaningful discussions and decisions.

♂ Mars' harmonious trine with Saturn brings a sense of discipline and determination to your actions. It's like a cosmic green light for pursuing your goals with structure and perseverance. Your energy is channeled effectively, enabling you to tackle challenges methodically and achieve lasting results.

☽ As the Moon moves into vibrant Leo, your emotions take on a more expressive and theatrical quality.

FEBRUARY WEEK TWO

⚡ The Sun's square with Uranus electrifies the atmosphere with unexpected twists and turns. This cosmic clash may bring sudden changes and disruptions to your plans. Flexibility and adaptability will be your allies during this period of unpredictability.

🌕 The Full Moon illuminates the night sky, marking a time of culmination and completion. It's a moment to celebrate your achievements and release what no longer serves you. Emotions may run high, and revelations may surface, guiding you toward necessary transformations.

🌙 As the Moon shifts into analytical Virgo, your focus turns toward practicality and attention to detail. You'll find satisfaction in organization and routine, making it an ideal time to tackle tasks that require precision.

💜 On Valentine's Day, Mercury gracefully ingresses into empathetic Pisces, infusing your thoughts and communication with compassion and sensitivity. A cosmic embrace encourages heartfelt expressions of love and understanding in your relationships. During this period, the power of empathy and intuition is magnified, making it sublime to connect emotionally.

FEBRUARY WEEK THREE

☽ When the Moon gracefully enters harmonious Libra, it's as if your emotions find their rhythm in the sweet melodies of balance and diplomacy. Relationships take center stage as you strive to create an atmosphere of fairness and mutual understanding. The beauty of art and aesthetics may also hold a special allure, encouraging you to surround yourself with visually pleasing elements that soothe your soul.

☽ As the Moon transitions into the depths of Scorpio, your emotional landscape takes on a profound and enigmatic quality. It's as if the cosmic spotlight is turned inward, inviting you to explore the hidden realms of your psyche. Your intuition becomes heightened, and you may uncover deep-seated truths and desires lurking beneath the surface. This phase encourages emotional authenticity, urging you to embrace the full spectrum of your feelings.

☉ With the Sun's graceful entrance into Pisces, you embark on a journey of heightened sensitivity and artistic inspiration. During this mystical phase, you'll find solace in creative and spiritual pursuits.

FEBRUARY WEEK THREE

As the Moon ventures into adventurous Sagittarius, your emotions take flight with an enthusiastic spirit of exploration. You'll be drawn to new experiences involving travel, education, or philosophical insights. This cosmic shift ignites your optimism and desire for expansion, encouraging you to venture beyond your comfort zone to pursue wisdom and personal growth.

Mercury's square with expansive Jupiter infuses your communication with enthusiasm and idealism. Your ideas may soar to great heights, driven by boundless optimism. However, balancing your visionary thinking with a practical approach is essential. This cosmic aspect reminds you that while dreaming big is necessary, a solid plan and grounded execution are equally vital for success. This aspect encourages you to think big and pay attention to the finer details. Avoid the temptation to overpromise or overcommit, as ensuring that your lofty plans align with your resources and capabilities is essential. Balancing your visionary thinking with a grounded approach will lead to more successful outcomes in both personal and professional endeavors.

FEBRUARY WEEK FOUR

🌙 As the Moon gracefully transitions into the diligent sign of Capricorn, your emotional landscape takes on a more grounded and responsible tone. You'll find yourself naturally inclined to focus on long-term goals, practical matters, and the structures that support your life. During this lunar phase, achieving a sense of discipline and organization is paramount, and you may feel a strong desire to tackle tasks that require commitment and perseverance.

🔴 Mars, the planet of action and motivation, makes a significant shift as it turns direct. After introspection and evaluation, the cosmic traffic light switches to green, and your drive and ambitions are reignited. This planetary change marks a decisive moment for moving forward with your plans, putting your intentions into action, and breaking free from obstacles.

🌙 The Moon's transition into the intellectually stimulating sign of Aquarius encourages a spirit of innovation and a desire to break free from convention. You'll be drawn to activities that promote originality and individuality, and social interactions may involve lively discussions and a shared vision for a brighter future.

FEBRUARY WEEK FOUR

◐ Mercury's conjunction with Saturn symbolizes a period of focused and disciplined thinking. This cosmic alignment emphasizes the importance of careful planning and attention to detail in your communication and mental pursuits. It's a time when your thoughts are structured and well-organized, allowing you to tackle complex tasks and engage in serious discussions with clarity and precision.

◐ Mercury's sextile with Uranus adds a touch of excitement and intellectual curiosity to your conversations and thought processes. Your mind is open to innovative ideas, and you may experience flashes of insight and inspiration. This cosmic connection encourages change and new possibilities in your thinking and communication. It's a time to embrace your uniqueness and break from constraints.

● The New Moon marks a fresh beginning and an opportunity to set new intentions. This lunar phase invites you to plant the seeds of your desires and envision the future you wish to create. It's a moment of renewal, making it ideal for growth and transformation.

MARCH WEEK ONE

☽ As Venus, the planet of love and harmony, turns retrograde, a reflective period in matters of the heart begins. It's a time to revisit past relationships, reevaluate your values, and reflect on the depth of your emotional connections. While this period may bring some challenges, it also provides an opportunity for inner growth and a deeper understanding of your desires.

☌ Mercury's conjunction with Neptune invites you to explore the realms of imagination and intuition. During this cosmic alignment, your mind may be more open to artistic and creative pursuits. You may find it easier to express yourself through poetry, music, or other forms of artistic communication. However, balancing your idealism with practicality is essential to avoid confusion in your thoughts and conversations.

⚡ The Sun's square with Jupiter encourages optimism and enthusiasm but may also bring the risk of overextending yourself. While your ambitions and confidence may be high, it's crucial to maintain a sense of realism and not take on too much. This aspect encourages you to balance your desire for expansion with a practical approach to achieving your goals.

MARCH WEEK ONE

Mercury's entrance into assertive Aries marks a period of direct and proactive communication. Your thoughts and words are more straightforward and to the point, making it an excellent time for making decisions and taking quick action. You may find yourself speaking your mind with greater confidence and assertiveness.

As the Moon transitions into inquisitive Gemini, your curiosity and desire for communication are heightened. It's an ideal time for engaging in social interactions, learning, and intellectual pursuits.

Mercury's sextile with transformative Pluto brings depth and intensity to your communication and thinking processes. You're unafraid to explore profound topics and may experience moments of powerful insight. This cosmic connection encourages you to delve into the mysteries of the mind and communicate authentically and deeply.

The Moon's move into nurturing Cancer brings a strong focus on emotional well-being and home life. You may feel a deep family connection and loved ones, and your emotional sensitivity heightens.

MARCH WEEK TWO

☼ When the Sun forms a harmonious trine with Mars, your energy and motivation align seamlessly. It's as if you have a cosmic boost of vitality and drive. This cosmic aspect encourages you to take action, making it an excellent time to tackle projects or pursue your goals. Your inner fire burns brightly, propelling you forward.

☽ As the Moon graciously enters Leo, you'll shine with a desire for recognition and self-expression. Your emotions are bold and theatrical; you'll seek moments to showcase your creativity and charisma. It's a time to bask in the spotlight and enjoy life's pleasures.

☿ Mercury's conjunction with Venus enhances your communication with charm and grace. Your words are sweet, and your interactions are filled with diplomacy and harmony. It's a lovely aspect of romantic conversations and artistic expressions. Use this cosmic connection to connect with others on a heartfelt level.

☽ The Moon's transition into meticulous Virgo brings a focus on organization and practicality. This lunar phase encourages you to tackle tasks precisely and create a sense of order.

MARCH WEEK TWO

○ When the Sun forms a conjunction with Saturn, it's a time for discipline and responsibility. This cosmic connection encourages you to take a structured approach to your goals and commitments. While it may involve hard work and a sense of duty, the rewards of this diligent effort are long-lasting.

○ The Full Moon illuminates your achievements and long-term goals. It's a moment of celebration and reflection on your path. This lunar phase encourages you to assess your ambitions and ensure they align with your desires. It's time to release what no longer serves you and make room for new intentions.

⚡ The Sun's sextile with Uranus adds an element of surprise and innovation to your life. This aspect promotes positive changes and a willingness to embrace the unconventional. You're open to new experiences and may desire greater freedom and individuality.

☽ As the Moon enters the diplomatic sign of Libra, your emotions crave harmony. You'll seek compromise and fairness in your interactions, making it an ideal time to mend any imbalances in your connections with others.

MARCH WEEK THREE

🔄 Mercury's retrograde journey invites you to embark on a cosmic rewind, encouraging introspection and reflection. It's a time when the universe gently suggests that you look back. During this period, you may revisit old ideas, reconnect with familiar faces, and reevaluate your plans. While Mercury retrograde is often associated with communication challenges, it also offers a chance to refine your thoughts and gain clarity in areas that may have felt hazy.

🌙 As the Moon gracefully transitions into the enigmatic sign of Scorpio, your emotions take on a deep and reflective quality. It's as if you're delving into the mysteries of your inner world, uncovering hidden truths, and exploring the depths of your feelings. This lunar phase invites you to embrace transformation and connect with your intuition profoundly.

🌙 As the Moon continues its journey into adventurous Sagittarius, a sense of optimism and curiosity washes over you. This lunar phase encourages expanding horizons and embracing new experiences. The call of adventure is strong, and you may plan future journeys.

MARCH WEEK THREE

☉ When the Sun harmonizes with Neptune, your soul is bathed in ethereal and dreamy energies. A cosmic embrace invites you to explore your imagination and spiritual depths. During this alignment, the boundaries between the material world and the mystical realms become thinner, allowing for heightened intuition, creative inspiration, and acts of compassion.

☉ The Sun's ingress into Aries marks the Vernal Equinox, a time of balance and renewal. It starts a new astrological year, bringing vitality and a sense of fresh beginnings. The energy of Aries is assertive and pioneering, encouraging you to take the lead and pursue your desires with courage and determination.

♥ Venus' sextile with transformative Pluto adds a touch of intensity and depth to your relationships and passions. It's as if your heart yearns for profound connections and experiences. This cosmic connection encourages you to explore the depths of love and desire, allowing transformation and regeneration in matters of the heart. It's a time to embrace your passions and experience the richness of emotional connection.

MARCH WEEK FOUR

☽ As the Moon gracefully moves into Capricorn, the cosmic spotlight shifts to matters of responsibility and ambition. Your emotions are more grounded and pragmatic, urging you to focus on your duties and long-term goals. This lunar phase inspires a sense of purpose and determination, encouraging you to take charge of your life and diligently work towards your aspirations.

♣ The conjunction of the Sun and Venus paints a picture of romance and harmony. It's as if the universe orchestrates a serenade to your relationships and those you hold dear. During this period, your connections are adorned with affection and beauty, creating an ideal atmosphere to express your feelings and bask in the finer aspects of life.

✦ The Sun's sextile with Pluto bestows an extra layer of depth and intensity to your experiences. This celestial connection paves the way for transformation and empowerment. You are granted the opportunity to delve into the heart of your desires and initiate meaningful changes in your life, emerging stronger and wiser.

MARCH WEEK FOUR

💜 The conjunction of Venus and Neptune further amplifies the dreamy and romantic atmosphere. It's a period of heightened creativity and a strong desire to experience transcendent love and beauty. During this time, your imagination takes flight, and you may be drawn to artistic and spiritual pursuits that allow you to explore the ethereal.

🌑 As the Moon transitions into Aries, you'll feel a surge of energy and assertiveness. It's a cosmic call to action, inspiring you to take the lead, embrace challenges, and assert your desires with unwavering confidence.

🌑 The New Moon marks a fresh beginning and an opportunity to set new intentions. This lunar phase invites you to plant the seeds of your desires and envision the future you wish to create. It's a moment of renewal and a cosmic blank canvas on which to paint your aspirations and dreams.

🔱 With Neptune's ingress into Aries, a new era of dreams and spiritual exploration unfolds. This cosmic shift may inspire innovative and idealistic visions for the future, fostering a sense of renewal and individuality.

APRIL WEEK ONE

🏠 When the Moon shifts into Cancer, your emotional landscape becomes nurturing and sensitive. This lunar phase invites you to connect with your inner world and those close to your heart.

⚙ The sextile between Saturn and Uranus introduces a harmonious cosmic conversation between tradition and innovation. It's like the universe provides you with a balanced recipe for change. You'll be able to blend your long-standing principles with fresh, forward-thinking ideas, making this period favorable for progressive projects and transformative endeavors.

🚀 Mars's sextile with Uranus ignites dynamic energy and the desire for action. This alignment resembles a cosmic booster rocket, propelling you enthusiastically toward your goals.

🔨 The trine between Mars and Saturn forms a solid foundation for your actions. It's akin to a celestial architect and builder coming together to create something lasting. During this phase, your determination and discipline are enhanced, enabling you to take on demanding tasks and complete them.

APRIL WEEK ONE

◯ The sextile between the Sun and Jupiter radiates positivity and abundance. It's as if the universe is sprinkling stardust on your endeavors, bringing luck and expansion to your life. This alignment encourages you to seize opportunities and aim for your highest goals.

💜 Venus's trine with Mars adds a harmonious touch to your relationships and desires. This alignment is like a cosmic cupid, bringing harmony and balance to your romantic and social interactions. Your passions and affections flow smoothly, making it an ideal time for loving connections.

🧩 The conjunction of Venus and Saturn combines the energies of love and responsibility. Relationships are more intense during this period, and commitments are highlighted. It's a favorable time for strengthening bonds and making long-term plans.

🔄 Mercury's direct motion signals a shift in communication and decision-making. It's the cosmic green light that allows plans to move forward. Delays and miscommunications become infrequent, facilitating smoother interactions and clarity in your thinking.

APRIL WEEK TWO

✦ When Venus forms a sextile with Uranus, it's like a spark of inspiration in your romantic and creative life. This harmonious connection encourages you to embrace the unusual and experiment with novel approaches to love and aesthetics. You might find yourself drawn to people and experiences that are refreshingly different. This cosmic play is a time for romantic surprises and a unique appreciation for the unconventional.

☽ As the Moon gracefully enters Virgo, your emotions take on an air of practicality and precision. It's as if a cosmic organizer has taken over, and you're motivated to pay attention to the details in both your inner and outer world. This lunar phase is perfect for decluttering, organizing, and fine-tuning various aspects of your life.

💜 Transitioning into Libra, the Moon invites you to embrace harmony and balance in your relationships and emotional life. During this phase, you'll feel a deep desire for fairness and peaceful interactions. You may find yourself naturally playing the role of a peacemaker, seeking compromise and beauty in every connection.

APRIL WEEK TWO

 The Full Moon is like a cosmic spotlight, illuminating your achievements and goals. This lunar culmination is the time to acknowledge your progress and celebrate your successes. Emotions run high during a Full Moon, making it a potent moment to let go of what no longer serves you and embrace the culmination of your efforts.

 With Venus turning direct, the planet of love and beauty is back on track, revitalizing your relationships and sense of aesthetics. If you've felt like your romantic or creative life has been in a holding pattern, now's the time for a positive shift. Your appreciation for art, beauty, and the sweetness of love regains its natural flow.

 The Moon's ingress into Scorpio delves deep into emotion and transformation. During this time, your feelings may intensify as you seek to uncover hidden truths and explore the mysteries of existence. Your emotional intuition is heightened, guiding you to confront profound aspects of your inner world and embark on a journey of self-discovery.

APRIL WEEK THREE

☾ When Mercury and Neptune conjoin, it's as if your mind and intuition merge in a poetic dance. This alignment encourages dreamy and imaginative thinking. You may find yourself more in tune with your inner creativity and spirituality. It's an ideal time for artistic and intuitive pursuits.

🦁 With Mars entering fiery Leo, your actions and desires become bold and theatrical. You exude confidence and an appetite for recognition. It's a cosmic call to embrace your inner leader and express your passions with flair and enthusiasm.

☉ The Sun's ingress into Taurus marks a time of stability and grounded energy. It's as if you're firmly rooted in the material world, appreciating the sensory pleasures of life. Your focus shifts to security, financial stability, and the beauty of the physical world.

🎆 Mars's trine with Neptune blends the assertive energy of Mars with the dreamy and compassionate qualities of Neptune. This celestial fusion encourages you to pursue your desires with empathy and creativity. It's a time when you can channel energy into artistic endeavors.

APRIL WEEK THREE

🌷 Easter Sunday brings a sense of renewal and rebirth. It's a day of celebration and reflection, symbolizing the emergence of new life and hope. Whether you observe this day religiously or enjoy it as a time for spring festivities, it's a moment to embrace the themes of resurrection and growth.

💜 Venus's sextile with Uranus adds a touch of excitement to your love life and creative pursuits. This harmonious connection encourages you to embrace the unexpected and explore new ways of expressing affection. It's a time when unconventional relationships and artistic experiments flourish.

🔍 When Mercury forms a sextile with Pluto, your communication takes on a more profound and probing quality. This aspect enhances your ability to investigate and research, making it an ideal time for delving into complex subjects or uncovering hidden truths.

🌙 As the Moon transitions into Aquarius, your emotions become open-minded and forward-thinking. It's when you may feel more inclined to embrace unconventional ideas and seek a sense of community.

APRIL WEEK FOUR

☾ As the Moon gracefully glides into Pisces, your emotions become like the ebb and flow of the ocean. It's a moment of reflection and connection to the mystical realms.

✷ Sun square Pluto brings a potent burst of transformative energy. This aspect can stir up power struggles and intense emotions. It's when you may need to confront deep-seated issues and make significant changes in your life. While it can be challenging, it also offers opportunities for growth and empowerment.

♥ Venus conjunct Saturn is a cosmic alignment that brings stability and commitment to your relationships. It's a time when love becomes more enduring. Your emotional bonds strengthen, and you may make long-term commitments in your love life or creative pursuits.

◌ The Moon's shift into Aries ignites your passions and desire for action. You're ready to take on challenges with enthusiasm and courage. This lunar phase encourages you to be assertive and go after what you want, as it encourages boldness, confidence, and a desire to lead by example.

APRIL WEEK FOUR

🪓 When Mars opposes Pluto, it's like a celestial clash of titans. This intense aspect can lead to power struggles and conflicts but also provides the determination and courage to overcome obstacles. Be mindful of your actions during this time, as the potential for transformation and breakthroughs is high.

🌳 As the Moon moves into Taurus, your emotions seek stability and comfort. It's a time when you're drawn to life's simple pleasures, from good food to the beauty of nature. This lunar phase encourages you to slow down and savor the moment.

🌑 The New Moon marks a fresh start and a blank canvas. It's a time for setting intentions and planting the seeds of new beginnings. Use this lunar phase to focus on aspirations, as the energy supports starting fresh.

💧 Venus entering Aries infuses your love life and creative pursuits with fiery passion. This transit encourages you to take bold and assertive action in matters of the heart. Your desires become more direct and immediate, and you're not afraid to pursue what you want with enthusiasm.

MAY WEEK ONE

🌙 The Moon's entry into Cancer brings a gentle and nurturing energy to your emotions. You might find yourself more attuned to the needs of your loved ones and inclined to create a cozy, secure environment. This lunar phase encourages you to connect with your feelings and seek comfort in the familiar.

💜 Venus's conjunction with Neptune is like a cosmic love potion, infusing your relationships with enchantment and compassion. It's a time when love knows no bounds, and your heart is open to profound, soulful connections. This aspect encourages you to explore your creative and artistic side, making it an ideal period for expressing your deepest emotions through art, music, or other creative outlets.

🦁 When the Moon moves into Leo, your emotions take on a more dramatic and expressive quality. This lunar phase encourages self-expression, creativity, and a desire to take center stage.

🔄 Pluto's retrograde motion signifies a period of inner transformation and self-discovery. You may revisit deep-seated issues, patterns, and desires during this time.

MAY WEEK ONE

❋ Mercury's sextile with Jupiter brings a boost of optimism and mental clarity. Your communication is more positive, and you're open to new ideas and opportunities. This aspect supports learning, teaching, and sharing knowledge, making it an excellent time for intellectual pursuits and expanding your horizons.

☾ As the Moon enters Virgo, your emotions become grounded and practical. It is when you focus on the details and strive for order. You may find satisfaction in tackling tasks that require precision and organization. It's a period of productivity and service to others. This lunar phase encourages you to analyze, refine, and improve various aspects of your life, from work to health.

☌ Venus's sextile with Pluto adds depth and intensity to your relationships and creative pursuits. You're drawn to transformative experiences and may form solid and passionate connections. This aspect encourages you to explore the depths of love and express your desires with a magnetic allure. It's a time for profound emotional relationships and artistic endeavors that leave a lasting impact.

MAY WEEK TWO

As the Moon gracefully enters Libra, your emotions are bathed in the harmonious and diplomatic energy of this air sign. You're naturally drawn to balance and fairness, seeking harmony in your relationships and surroundings. This lunar phase encourages you to appreciate beauty, express your creativity, and find common ground in your interactions with others.

Mercury's ingress into Taurus brings a deliberate and practical tone to your communication style. Your words are grounded and purposeful, and you may find yourself drawn to discussions about material and financial matters. This planetary transit is when you value stability and tangible results in your conversations.

When the Moon transitions into passionate Scorpio, your emotions dive into the deep waters of intensity and transformation. It's when you're willing to explore the hidden realms of your psyche and relationships, seeking profound experiences. You may find yourself drawn to probing the mysteries of life and the confidential aspects of your psyche. This lunar phase encourages you to embrace change and release what no longer serves you.

MAY WEEK TWO

☾ The Full Moon is a powerful culmination and a time of release. It's like the climax of a cosmic story, where the intentions you set at the New Moon reach their peak. It's as if the cosmic spotlight shines on your achievements and brings clarity. This lunar phase encourages you to reflect on what you've initiated since the New Moon and adjust as needed. This lunar phase enables you to remember your progress and let go of what's no longer in alignment with your goals.

🔍 Mercury's square with Pluto intensifies your thinking and communication. It's as if your mind becomes a detective, delving deep into issues and uncovering hidden truths. While this aspect can bring powerful insights, it may also lead to power struggles in your conversations. Use this energy wisely, focusing on transformation and healing.

♐ As the Moon moves into adventurous Sagittarius, your emotions take on a more optimistic and free-spirited tone. It's a time when you seek adventure, exploration, and a broader perspective on life. This lunar phase encourages you to expand your horizons, embrace new experiences, and embrace your inner wanderlust.

MAY WEEK THREE

◾ As the Moon gracefully transitions into Capricorn, your emotions adopt a pragmatic and goal-oriented tone. You're inclined to focus on your responsibilities, career, and long-term objectives. This lunar phase encourages discipline and a strong sense of purpose, making it an ideal time for planning and working toward your ambitions.

⚡ The conjunction of the Sun and Uranus marks a dynamic and electrifying cosmic alignment. This event brings a surge of unexpected and innovative energy into your life. You may experience breakthroughs, sudden insights, or a strong desire for change and independence. It's a time to embrace your unique qualities and seek freedom.

◯ Mercury's square with Mars ignites your mental processes with fiery and assertive energy. Your thoughts are swift, but they can also become heated and impulsive. This aspect encourages passionate communication but may lead to arguments and hasty decisions. It's essential to channel this energy wisely.

MAY WEEK THREE

☽ As the Moon moves into Aquarius, your emotions take on a visionary quality. You're more open to unconventional ideas and humanitarian concerns. This lunar phase encourages social connections and a desire to contribute to the greater good. You seek intellectual stimulation and freedom of expression.

☉ The Sun's sextile with Saturn brings a stable and disciplined influence to your endeavors. You're more focused on your responsibilities and long-term goals, allowing you to make steady progress. This aspect encourages patience, structure, and a sense of accomplishment.

☽ As the Moon drifts into Pisces, your emotions become sensitive, intuitive, and deeply connected to the spiritual and emotional realms.

☉ The Sun's transition into Gemini marks a period of intellectual curiosity and increased communication. You're more inclined to engage in conversations, learn new things, and share ideas. This solar shift encourages adaptability and versatility, making it an excellent time for networking and exploring various interests.

MAY WEEK FOUR

💜 Venus's trine with Mars creates a harmonious dance of passion and desire. Your relationships and creative endeavors are infused with balance, making it easier to express your affections with grace and assertiveness. This aspect encourages the blending of feminine and masculine energies, fostering loving and harmonious connections.

 Mercury's conjunction with Uranus sparks innovation and sudden insights in your thinking and communication. It's a time when your mind is open to new ideas and original thoughts. You may experience breakthroughs and a desire to express your unique perspective.

 Saturn's ingress into Aries marks a significant shift in your life. It's like the cosmic taskmaster entering a new arena. During this transition, you're encouraged to take on challenges with a pioneering spirit and a sense of assertiveness. Your ambitions and leadership qualities come to the forefront.

 Mercury's move into Gemini enhances your mental agility and communication skills.

MAY WEEK FOUR

✏️ Mercury's sextile with Saturn provides a structured and disciplined approach to your thinking and communication. You're able to focus on essential tasks and convey your ideas with clarity and responsibility.

🌑 The New Moon marks a fresh beginning and an opportunity to set new intentions. It's like a cosmic reset button, giving you a chance to plant the seeds of your desires. This lunar phase encourages introspection and the formulation of new goals.

🔍 Mercury's trine with Pluto deepens your thinking and communication. You're drawn to profound conversations and have a keen ability to uncover hidden information and insights. This aspect encourages in-depth research and a desire to transform through the power of words.

📝 The Sun's conjunction with Mercury enhances your mental understanding and communication skills. Your mind is sharp, and you're able to express your thoughts with clarity and precision. This aspect encourages intellectual pursuits and effective self-expression.

JUNE WEEK ONE

♍ When the Moon gracefully enters Virgo, your emotions adopt a practical and analytical tone. You may find yourself paying closer attention to details and seeking perfection in your daily routines. This lunar phase encourages you to nurture and organize your life, promoting a sense of order and efficiency.

♎ As the Moon moves into Libra, your emotions seek balance, harmony, and connection with others. It's a time when you're more inclined to weigh the pros and cons of various situations, striving for fairness and cooperation in your relationships. This lunar phase encourages diplomacy and a desire to create beauty in your surroundings.

☽ Venus sextile Jupiter forms a delightful aspect that enhances your social life and sense of well-being. Your relationships and finances benefit from a touch of luck and optimism. This aspect encourages you to indulge in the pleasures of life, whether through enjoyable gatherings, travel, or artistic pursuits. It's a time when love and generosity flow freely, and opportunities for expansion and enjoyment abound.

JUNE WEEK ONE

✏ Mercury sextile Mars infuses your mental processes with energy and determination. You're ready to express your ideas with confidence and take action on your plans. This aspect encourages effective communication and the ability to tackle tasks with vigor. You're more persuasive and ready to take action on your ideas. This aspect promotes effective decision-making and dynamic discussions.

☽ Venus's ingress into Taurus brings a sensual and earthy quality to your relationships and pleasures. You're drawn to the comforts of life, seeking stability and beauty in your surroundings. This transit encourages you to savor simple pleasures, indulge in delicious food, and connect with nature.

🌑 When the Moon delves into Scorpio, your emotions take on an intense and transformative tone. You may find yourself delving into the mysteries of life and your innermost desires. This lunar phase encourages self-reflection, healing, and a deep connection to the hidden realms of your psyche. It's a time when you seek authenticity and may be drawn to investigate hidden truths.

JUNE WEEK TWO

🤝 Mercury's conjunction with Jupiter expands your mental horizons and encourages positive thinking. It's a time when your mind is open to new possibilities, and you're eager to learn and share knowledge. This aspect can enhance communication, making it an excellent time for negotiations, teaching, and exploring big ideas.

🦀 Mercury's move into Cancer brings a more emotional and intuitive approach to your thinking and communication. Your words are infused with empathy and a deep understanding of others' feelings. This transit encourages discussions about home and family matters and can foster more nurturing connections with those you care about.

🔧 Mercury's square with Saturn adds a touch of practicality and discipline to your thinking. It's a time when you may encounter challenges in communication or encounter obstacles in your plans. However, this aspect also provides an opportunity for structured thinking and attention to detail.

🌋 Venus square Pluto can bring intensity and transformation to your relationships and desires.

JUNE WEEK TWO

Jupiter's ingress into Cancer marks a shift towards expansion in emotional and home-related matters. You may seek a sense of security and well-being in your personal life and family. This transit encourages nurturing and growth in your domestic sphere, possibly through a focus on home improvements or strengthening family bonds.

The Full Moon is a culmination of energy, illuminating the results of your efforts and intentions from the past month. It's a time of heightened emotions and a potential turning point. This lunar phase encourages you to celebrate achievements and make any necessary adjustments to your goals and projects.

Mercury's sextile with Venus enhances your ability to express love and affection. Your words are filled with charm and grace, making it an excellent time for heartfelt conversations and harmonious interactions in your relationships. This aspect encourages socializing and enjoying the beauty in life.

As the Moon moves into Capricorn, your emotions adopt a practical and responsible tone.

JUNE WEEK THREE

⚡ Mars square Uranus creates an atmosphere of tension and unpredictability. It's like a cosmic clash between the warrior and the rebel. This aspect encourages you to find a balance between your desire for action and the need for stability in your life. Be cautious and think before you act to avoid impulsive decisions.

🏛 Jupiter square Saturn represents a conflict between expansion and restriction. It's as if the cosmic teacher meets the taskmaster. This aspect encourages you to strike a balance between your ambitions and the practical limitations you face. It's a time for responsible growth and long-term planning.

🌙 The Moon's ingress into Pisces brings a dreamy and intuitive quality to your emotions. It's like a cosmic lullaby, encouraging introspection, empathy, and a connection to the mystical realms.

🛠 Mars's move into Virgo shifts your focus toward practical action and attention to detail. You'll find satisfaction in taking care of daily tasks and perfecting your skills. This transit encourages you to channel your energy into organized and productive endeavors.

JUNE WEEK THREE

🔺 As the Moon enters Aries, your emotions take on an assertive and pioneering quality. It's like a cosmic spark igniting your passion and drive. This lunar phase encourages you to be more self-reliant, courageous, and ready to take on challenges with enthusiasm.

♃ Jupiter square Neptune is a complex aspect that blurs the boundaries between reality and illusion. It's like a cosmic tug-of-war between your ideals and the practical world. This aspect encourages you to be mindful of potential delusions or over-optimism while still holding onto your dreams and spiritual beliefs.

🌷 The Moon's ingress into Taurus brings a grounded and sensual quality to your emotions. This lunar phase encourages you to connect with the physical world, whether through enjoying good food, appreciating art, or finding serenity in nature.

☀ The Sun's ingress into Cancer marks the June Solstice, a time when daylight is at its peak in the Northern Hemisphere. It's a turning point in the year, emphasizing themes of family, home, and emotional well-being.

JUNE WEEK FOUR

When the Sun squares Saturn, you may encounter challenges and obstacles that test your patience and perseverance. It's like a cosmic reality check, reminding you of your responsibilities and limitations. This aspect encourages you to approach your goals with discipline.

The Sun's square to Neptune can bring a sense of confusion or disillusionment. It's like a cosmic fog, making it challenging to see things clearly. This aspect encourages you to be cautious in your decisions and take time for reflection to avoid deception or self-deception.

The Sun's conjunction with Jupiter is a powerful aspect that fills you with optimism and a sense of abundance. It's like a cosmic blessing, expanding your opportunities and encouraging a positive outlook. This aspect invites you to explore new horizons and embrace the potential for growth and success.

The New Moon represents a fresh beginning, a clean slate for setting intentions and launching new projects. It's like a cosmic blank page, ready for you to write the next chapter of your life. This lunar phase encourages you to set clear goals and manifest your desires.

JUNE WEEK FOUR

◐ The Sun's sextile with Mars infuses you with vigor and assertiveness. It's like a cosmic energy boost, motivating you to take action and move forward with your plans. This aspect encourages you to channel your drive and passion productively.

☿ As Mercury moves into Leo, your thoughts become more expressive and bold. You'll feel more inclined to share your ideas with confidence and charisma. This transit encourages creativity and a flair for dramatic or persuasive communication.

♄ Mercury's trine with Saturn offers stability and a structured approach to your mental processes. It's like a cosmic anchor, grounding your thoughts and helping you make practical decisions. This aspect encourages responsible and disciplined thinking.

♆ Mercury's trine with Neptune enhances your intuition and creativity. It's like a cosmic flow of inspiration, allowing you to tap into your imagination and empathy. This aspect encourages artistic expression and a deeper connection to your dreams and inner wisdom.

JULY WEEK ONE

💜 Venus conjunct Uranus brings a taste of excitement and unpredictability to your relationships and pleasures. It's a cosmic spark in matters of the heart, encouraging you to embrace the unexpected and try new things. This aspect can lead to exciting encounters and a desire for greater freedom in your love life.

♊ Venus's move into Gemini introduces a more playful and curious energy to your relationships and social life. It's a cosmic breeze that encourages light-hearted connections and a variety of interests. This transit enhances communication in love and stimulates a desire for mental stimulation in partnerships.

🌀 Neptune turning retrograde signifies a period of inner reflection and spiritual development. It's a cosmic call to revisit your dreams and ideals, reconnect with your inner self, and gain clarity on your spiritual path. This retrograde period encourages you to discern between illusion and intuition.

💍 Venus sextile Saturn brings stability and commitment to your relationships and creative pursuits. It's a cosmic anchor that helps you build security.

JULY WEEK ONE

♀ Venus sextile Neptune adds a touch of enchantment and romance to your interactions and artistic endeavors. It's a cosmic spell that deepens your emotional connections and enhances your creative inspiration. This aspect encourages sensitivity, empathy, and a desire to infuse your art with a sense of the divine.

♐ The Moon's ingress into Sagittarius brings a more adventurous and optimistic tone to your emotions. This lunar phase inspires a love of learning and a spirit of exploration.

⚡ Uranus's move into Gemini marks a shift in communication and ideas. It's like a cosmic wake-up call to embrace innovation, change, and intellectual exploration. This transit encourages a more diverse and eclectic approach to sharing ideas.

🖤 Venus trine Pluto deepens your emotional connections and intensifies your desires. It's like a cosmic magnetism that draws you to profound and transformative experiences in love and creativity. This aspect encourages you to explore the depths of your passions and forge solid and enduring bonds.

JULY WEEK TWO

🌙 When the Moon gracefully moves into Capricorn, you'll find your emotional focus shifts toward the pragmatic aspects of life. It's as if a cosmic executive takes the reins, encouraging you to set goals, exercise discipline, and approach your feelings with a structured mindset. This lunar phase is ideal for taking on responsibilities, making plans, and tending to your ambitions. Your emotions are channeled into achieving your long-term objectives, and you may feel a strong need for order and control.

🌕 The Full Moon represents the culmination of a lunar cycle, and it's a celestial event that amplifies your emotions. This phase encourages you to reflect on your progress, celebrate your successes, and release what no longer serves you. The Full Moon is a powerful time for letting go, forgiveness, and completing projects.

🌙 As the Moon shifts into Aquarius, a sense of independence and innovation permeates your emotional landscape. It's like a cosmic rebel is awakened within you, urging you to explore unique and unconventional experiences. During this phase, you may be drawn to social causes, group activities, or unusual friendships.

JULY WEEK TWO

♐ Saturn turning retrograde initiates a period of introspection and review, particularly concerning your responsibilities and long-term goals. It's like a cosmic teacher inviting you to revisit your life's structure, ensuring it aligns with your true desires and ambitions. During this retrograde, you may find yourself reevaluating your commitments, career path, and the structures you've built. It's a time for inner reflection, adjusting your plans, and fine-tuning your ambitions for a more authentic and fulfilling life.

☾ With the Moon's journey into Pisces, a wave of sensitivity and empathy washes over you. It's as if a cosmic artist paints your emotions with vivid and dreamy hues, encouraging you to delve deep into your inner world. During this phase, you may find that your intuition is heightened, and you're more attuned to the emotions of others. Compassion and a desire to assist those in need may become more pronounced. It's a spiritually charged time for introspection, creative expression, and connecting with the profound depths of your soul.

JULY WEEK THREE

🌙 When the Moon makes its entrance into Aries, there's a palpable surge of energy in your emotional landscape. It's like a cosmic call to action, a rally for your inner warrior to take the reins. During this lunar phase, you'll find yourself encouraged with a newfound sense of daring. It's the perfect moment to embrace your adventurous side and seize the day with fiery enthusiasm. In Aries' spirited company, your emotions become a driving force, propelling you toward your desires and igniting a passion for life's endeavors.

🔄 Mercury's retrograde motion ushers in a phase of profound introspection and contemplation. It's as though a cosmic librarian has asked you to revisit the shelves of your mind and reexamine the stories written in your thoughts and words. During this celestial event, you'll find yourself retracing mental steps, clarifying misunderstandings, and fine-tuning the symphony of your ideas. While Mercury may appear to move backward in the sky, its influence encourages you to move forward, armed with greater clarity and awareness.

JULY WEEK THREE

💗 Mercury's harmonious sextile with Venus creates a celestial bridge between your mind and heart as if they've decided to waltz together in perfect unison. During this phase, your thoughts and feelings align with an exquisite balance that evokes sweet and meaningful communication. This celestial embrace is an ideal time for heartfelt conversations, sharing your affections, and connecting with others in ways that feel harmonious and genuinely heartfelt. It's a period where your words resonate with the melody of your emotions.

With the Moon's graceful transition into Gemini, your emotions take on a curious and communicative flair. It's as if a cosmic storyteller awakens within you, compelling you to express your thoughts, feelings, and ideas with vivacity and zeal. During this lunar phase, your intellectual curiosity is piqued, prompting a desire to connect with others through engaging and enlightening conversations. Gemini's influence encourages you to explore the world of ideas and exchange insights with those who share your love for the beauty of words. It's a journey of self-discovery and connection, enriching your relationship with the world around you.

JULY WEEK FOUR

When the Sun forms a harmonious sextile with Uranus, it's as if the universe is encouraging you to infuse some excitement and innovation into your life. This cosmic connection between the luminary of self and the planet of change sparks inspiration and a desire to break free from routine. It's an excellent time to explore new interests, experiment with fresh ideas, and infuse your daily life with a touch of unpredictability.

The Sun's harmonious trine with Saturn brings a sense of discipline and structure to your endeavors. It's as if a cosmic mentor is guiding your efforts, ensuring that you build upon a solid foundation. With the Sun and Saturn in alignment, you're well-equipped to accomplish your ambitions and earn recognition for your hard work.

The Sun's trine with Neptune is like a gateway to the dreamy, ethereal realms of your imagination. This cosmic connection allows you to blend your creativity with a deep sense of compassion and intuition. During this time, your empathy and artistic talents flourish, making it an ideal phase for creative projects and acts of kindness. It's a moment when you can find inspiration in the subtleties of life as your spiritual sense rises.

JULY WEEK FOUR

🌑 The arrival of a New Moon signals a fresh start, like turning the page of a cosmic diary. This lunar phase encourages you to set intentions and plant the seeds of your desires. It's a moment of introspection and clarity when you can shape your future. As the Moon wanes and then waxes into a new cycle, your intentions will grow just as you nurture the growth of a new plant.

🌑 When the Sun opposes Pluto, it's like a tug-of-war between the self and transformation. This aspect brings intense power struggles and a deep dive into the hidden aspects of your personality. While it can be challenging, it also offers a profound opportunity for self-discovery and rebirth. Your desires and motivations are under scrutiny, and you're called to confront and release what no longer serves your growth.

☺ With Venus gracefully moving into Cancer, your approach to love and relationships becomes nurturing and emotionally driven. Venus, the planet of love, seeks comfort and emotional connection during this transit. You'll find that your affections are deeply tied to feelings of security and belonging.

AUGUST WEEK ONE

💔 When Venus squares Saturn, a celestial tug of war between love and responsibility unfolds. It's as if the cosmos has you standing at a crossroads, torn between the desire for romantic connections and the weight of your commitments. This aspect can introduce a sense of restriction into your relationships, making it crucial to find a delicate equilibrium between emotional fulfillment and practical duties. By embracing the challenges presented by this aspect, you can build stronger, more enduring connections.

🌙 Venus square Neptune adds an extra layer of complexity to matters of the heart. This aspect may lead to moments of confusion or even idealization, where your emotions may not align with the actual circumstances. Trusting your intuition and taking a grounded approach to love is essential during this time, ensuring your feelings are rooted in authenticity rather than illusion.

♐ With the Moon's ingress into Sagittarius, your emotional landscape takes on an adventurous and free-spirited hue. This lunar placement encourages you to actively seek opportunities for growth and learning.

AUGUST WEEK ONE

🌑 As the Moon transitions into Capricorn, a more pragmatic and duty-driven emotional energy takes hold. It's akin to the universe prompting you to focus on your responsibilities and long-term goals. During this phase, you'll derive satisfaction from accomplishing tasks, making progress in your professional life, and ensuring that your ambitions are on a steady and structured path.

♎ Mars's ingress into Libra introduces a newfound sense of equilibrium and diplomacy to your actions. This cosmic shift encourages you to approach conflicts with grace and cooperation, seeking resolutions that promote harmony. Your efforts to create and maintain equilibrium in your personal and professional life are well-supported under this cosmic influence.

This week's celestial movements weave a tapestry of intricate emotions, responsibilities, dreams, and the pursuit of balance. While you may grapple with moments of uncertainty, each of these aspects offers an opportunity for growth. Embrace the spirited nature of Sagittarius, find practical solutions during the Capricorn lunar phase, and gracefully navigate the intricate dance between love and responsibility.

AUGUST WEEK TWO

✸ When Mars forms a trine with Uranus, it's like igniting a cosmic firecracker of innovation and action. This dynamic aspect brings a surge of energy and a desire for change. You'll find yourself motivated to break free from routines and embrace new, exciting challenges. This harmonious alignment encourages you to trust your instincts and harness your determination for transformative endeavors.

✷ However, the opposition between Mars and Saturn creates a cosmic tug-of-war between assertiveness and caution. It's as if you're navigating the tricky terrain of pushing forward while keeping a watchful eye on potential obstacles. Saturn's influence may introduce some delays or challenges, but this aspect also offers valuable lessons in discipline and patience.

● A Full Moon signifies a culmination, and it's like the universe's spotlight shines brightly on your emotions and intentions. This phase can bring things to a head, whether in your personal life or on a larger scale. Feelings run high during a Full Moon, making it a potent moment for clarity, revelation, and resolution.

AUGUST WEEK TWO

Mars trine Pluto fuels your ambitions and empowers you to transform your life in profound ways. This aspect is a force of determination, resilience, and intense focus. You'll find yourself driven to uncover hidden truths and make significant changes. It's a powerful alignment for personal growth and empowerment. With Pluto's influence, you can tap into deep reservoirs of strength and push through obstacles with unwavering determination.

Mercury's direct motion marks the end of a retrograde period, bringing a sigh of relief for communication and decision-making. The cosmic traffic jam in your mind begins to clear, and you can move forward with plans and projects that have been delayed.

When Venus conjuncts Jupiter, it's as if the cosmic lovers come together in a joyful embrace. This aspect is a harmonious alignment of love, beauty, and abundance. You'll feel a surge of optimism, generosity, and an open heart. It's a time when relationships can thrive, and financial opportunities may appear. This conjunction encourages you to savor life's pleasures and share your good fortune with others.

AUGUST WEEK THREE

⚡ When Mercury and Mars align in a harmonious sextile, it's as if the cosmic gears of communication and action are turning effortlessly in your favor. Your thoughts are like well-sharpened tools, and your words become potent instruments for practical expression. It's a time when your mind and your actions are in perfect sync, allowing you to tackle tasks with clarity and enthusiasm. This alignment not only sharpens your intellect but also ignites your assertiveness, making it an ideal period for tackling challenges head-on and initiating productive conversations.

🌙 With the Moon gracefully traversing through the versatile sign of Gemini, your mental faculties are in full bloom. Your curiosity is piqued, and you find yourself more open to the vast realm of knowledge and ideas around you. It's like a cosmic invitation to embark on a mental adventure, whether that's through reading, learning, or engaging in fascinating conversations. Your adaptability is heightened, making it an excellent time to explore new horizons and expand your intellectual horizons.

AUGUST WEEK THREE

✦ The encore performance of Mercury's sextile to Mars reinforces your ability to communicate and act with precision. Your words resonate with conviction, and your thoughts are channeled into effective problem-solving. This cosmic tag team lends you the energy to confront challenges with determination, ensuring that your ideas are heard and respected.

As the Moon moves into Cancer, emotions rise to the forefront. The nurturing energy of Cancer imbues your surroundings with a comforting and empathetic atmosphere. It's a time for fostering profound connections with family and loved ones as the urge to care for those close to your heart becomes paramount.

The Moon's passage through radiant Leo brings a sense of playfulness and creativity into your life. You're inclined to shine in the spotlight, whether it's through artistic expression, leadership, or simply sharing your unique talents with the world. It's a cosmic invitation to embrace your inner child, infuse joy into your endeavors, and take center stage in your creative pursuits. Let your light shine, and let your heart be your guide during this period of self-expression.

AUGUST WEEK FOUR

☀ As the Sun gracefully glides into Virgo, it ushers in a time of increased focus on details, organization, and practicality. You'll find yourself inclined to pay attention to the finer points and make constructive improvements. This solar influence encourages you to embrace a more structured and systematic approach to life, making it a perfect period for tackling tasks that demand precision and efficiency.

🌑 The arrival of the New Moon signals a fresh beginning, a blank canvas on which to paint your aspirations and intentions. It is a potent time to set new goals, launch projects, and align your energy with what you hope to achieve. The seeds you plant during this lunar phase have the potential to grow and flourish in the coming weeks, so make the most of this cosmic opportunity to manifest your desires.

⚡ The Sun's square to Uranus ignites a burst of electrifying energy, bringing unexpected twists and turns to your life. This aspect encourages you to break free from routine and embrace change. While it might feel a bit unsettling, it's a chance to step out of your comfort zone and explore new horizons.

AUGUST WEEK FOUR

💜 Venus graces Leo with her presence, infusing your relationships and creative pursuits with a touch of drama and passion. You'll radiate confidence and charisma during this time, making it an ideal period for socializing and expressing your unique style. Your inner artist shines brightly, and you may find inspiration in the arts or creative endeavors.

🌙 Venus's trine to Saturn brings stability and commitment to your relationships. You'll find it easier to make long-term commitments, and existing partnerships may deepen. It is a time when your sense of responsibility enhances your emotional connections.

🪐 Venus's sextile to Uranus adds a delightful spark of novelty and excitement to your love life and finances. Unexpected encounters and financial opportunities may arise, bringing a sense of adventure and spontaneity.

🌊 Venus's trine to Neptune infuses your relationships and artistic endeavors with dreamy and imaginative energy. It's a time of heightened creativity and a deep connection to the spiritual and emotional aspects of your experiences.

SEPTEMBER WEEK ONE

As Saturn moves into Pisces, its entrance marks a profound shift in the cosmic landscape. In this watery realm, Saturn's stern and structured energy takes on a more empathetic and intuitive tone. Your focus turns inward, and you're prompted to explore the depths of your emotions. You may find yourself more attuned to the subtleties of life, making it an ideal period for introspection and nurturing your compassionate side.

Mercury's journey into Virgo brings a keen eye for detail and precision to your thought processes. You'll find yourself naturally inclined to analyze, organize, and categorize. It's an excellent phase for tasks that require meticulous attention, problem-solving, and fine-tuning. This transit encourages a structured approach to your communication and daily routines.

When Mercury squares Uranus, it's like a lightning bolt of inspiration. This aspect encourages flexibility and adaptability in your thinking. Be open to sudden flashes of insight and embrace change, even if it disrupts your mental routines. It's a time for breaking free from old patterns and exploring new horizons.

SEPTEMBER WEEK ONE

♂ The Mars Jupiter square fuels your desire for growth and adventure. You're imbued with a surge of energy and enthusiasm, making this a period where you might aim for the stars. However, it's crucial to strike a balance between ambition and overextension. Pace yourself and set achievable goals to make the most of this dynamic energy.

🔄 Uranus turning retrograde invites you to turn your gaze inward. This retrograde period encourages reflection on the changes and innovations you've encountered in recent months. It's a time for integrating these newfound insights and revisiting your quest for liberation. Delve into your inner world to unlock the next phase of your unique journey.

🌝 The Full Moon is the crescendo of this celestial symphony. It's a time of culmination and realization, where the intentions you set during the previous New Moon come to fruition. Emotions may run high during this phase, providing an opportunity for self-awareness and profound insights. Embrace this opportunity for personal growth and self-discovery, allowing the universe's cosmic dance to guide your path.

SEPTEMBER WEEK TWO

☾ The Moon's ingress into Aries ushers in a period of passionate and spontaneous emotions. You'll feel a surge of enthusiasm and a strong desire to take the lead. It is ideal to initiate new projects, embrace your assertiveness, and follow your instincts. Aries' energy empowers you to be more direct and courageous in pursuing your goals.

☾ Transitioning into Taurus, the Moon brings a sense of stability and practicality to your emotional landscape. During this phase, you'll seek comfort and security in your surroundings. It's an opportune moment to indulge in life's sensual pleasures, focus on financial matters, and appreciate the beauty that surrounds you. The Taurus Moon encourages you to ground and center.

☉ The Sun's harmonious sextile with Jupiter is like a cosmic blessing, showering you with optimism and opportunity. This alignment expands your horizons and infuses your life with a sense of abundance. It's the perfect time to set ambitious goals, explore new territories, and approach challenges with confidence and enthusiasm. This aspect encourages you to dream big and make your aspirations a reality.

SEPTEMBER WEEK TWO

With the Moon entering communicative Gemini, your curiosity and sociability soar. You'll find yourself eager to connect with others, engage in stimulating conversations, and expand your knowledge. The Gemini Moon fuels your intellectual curiosity.

Mercury's harmonious sextile with Jupiter enhances your communication skills and intellectual prowess. This cosmic aspect supercharges your ability to articulate your ideas, make plans, and engage in meaningful discussions. It's a period when your thoughts flow with ease, and your optimism shines brightly. Take advantage of this time to embark on new educational endeavors and explore opportunities for personal growth.

When the Sun conjoins Mercury, your thoughts and self-expression align seamlessly. This powerful conjunction sharpens your intellect and communication abilities, making it an excellent time for important conversations, negotiations, and decision-making. Clarity and mental precision are at your disposal, enabling you to express yourself with confidence and efficiency.

SEPTEMBER WEEK THREE

☀ The delightful sextile between Venus and Mars opens the door to a period of harmonious coexistence between love and desire. During this time, your relationships and passions are likely to flourish, fostering cooperation and affectionate connections in your romantic life.

☿ Nevertheless, Mercury's opposition to the stern Saturn might introduce communication challenges. These cosmic forces could lead to difficulties in expressing your thoughts clearly or encountering demanding conversations. To navigate this aspect, patience and careful consideration are your best allies.

☀ As Mercury gracefully glides into diplomatic Libra, it ushers in a balanced and cooperative atmosphere for your interactions. This ingress is an excellent time for resolving conflicts, as you naturally seek harmony and understanding in your conversations.

☾ Mercury's opposition with Neptune, however, casts a dreamy, at times confusing, veil over your thoughts and discussions. It's important to stay vigilant against misunderstandings and ensure that details are well-sorted in your conversations.

SEPTEMBER WEEK THREE

🚀 Mercury's trine with both Uranus and Pluto brings a surge of intellectual brilliance and transformative insights. This aspect enhances your mental agility and adaptability, empowering you to break free from conventional thinking and embrace innovative ideas.

❀ With Venus entering pragmatic Virgo, you'll find pleasure in attending to the finer details of your relationships.

⚡ On the other hand, the square between Venus and Uranus introduces an element of unpredictability to your relationships. This aspect may spark unexpected changes or lead to encounters with unconventional romantic interests.

☉ The Sun's opposition with responsible Saturn may pose challenges in terms of self-expression and personal authority. You could encounter obstacles that demand patience and determination to overcome.

🌑 With the arrival of the New Moon, a fresh beginning dawns. This lunar event provides an opportunity to set new intentions, embark on a journey of self-discovery, and nurture personal growth.

SEPTEMBER WEEK FOUR

💧 As Mars enters Scorpio, you're about to embark on a passionate and determined journey. This celestial alignment infuses you with an intense drive and the urge to dig deep into your desires and ambitions. The energy is magnetic and transformative, encouraging you to tackle challenges with unwavering determination. It's a time to take bold action and confront obstacles head-on, knowing that you have the inner strength to persevere.

☺ The September Equinox marks a moment of balance and transition in the cosmic calendar. Just as the seasons shift, this period calls for a reassessment of your life's equilibrium. It's an opportunity to realign with your goals, shed what no longer serves you, and embrace the changing tides of life. As nature adapts to new conditions, you must adjust to the evolving circumstances in your journey, too.

♎ With the Sun's entrance into Libra, the focus turns to your relationships. You'll find yourself naturally drawn to seek harmony and fairness in all your interactions. The energy of this period encourages you to address any imbalances in your personal and professional connections. It's an ideal time to mend bridges.

SEPTEMBER WEEK FOUR

However, as the Sun opposes Neptune, there's a touch of illusion in the air. While your intentions are noble, it's essential to maintain clarity and discernment. This aspect reminds you not to idealize situations or individuals too much. Be cautious about falling into the trap of wishful thinking, and instead, approach matters with a grounded perspective.

The Sun's trines with Uranus and Pluto bring an electrifying blend of transformation and innovation to your life. During this period, you'll find yourself more open to change and receptive to new ideas and experiences. You become adaptable and resilient, ready to embrace the transformative power of the universe.

As the Moon enters Scorpio, it's a time for deep emotional exploration. Your feelings and motivations take on a reflective quality, encouraging you to dive into your inner world. It's a period of self-discovery and understanding the driving forces behind your actions.

The square between Mars and Pluto can intensify power struggles and conflicts. Avoid confrontations and seek common ground to resolve differences.

OCTOBER WEEK ONE

🌙 When the Moon ventures into the intellectual realm of Aquarius, it's as if your mind gets a breath of fresh air. You're infused with a desire for freedom and a yearning to break away from the ordinary. This ingress is the time to embrace unconventional ideas and get involved in humanitarian causes that speak to your heart. Your community and social circles may take on a more significant role as you seek like-minded individuals with whom you can share your visions. Your open-mindedness can lead to exciting collaborations and new experiences.

☿ However, as Mercury squares Jupiter, you might find yourself in a bit of a mental tug-of-war between details and grand, expansive thinking. On one hand, you're enthusiastic and optimistic about your ideas, and your mind is brimming with possibilities. On the other, there's a need for practicality and attention to the finer points. This cosmic shift is a call for balance - a reminder to infuse your grand visions with a dose of realism. Use your enthusiasm to fuel your efforts while also maintaining a sense of practicality to bring your plans to life.

OCTOBER WEEK ONE

☾ As the Moon gracefully glides into Pisces, the emotional landscape undergoes a dreamy transformation. Your feelings become more empathetic and compassionate, and you're naturally drawn to acts of kindness and understanding.

🚀 The Moon's entry into Aries marks a dynamic shift in energy. Your assertiveness and courage take center stage. You'll feel an inner fire and determination that propels you toward your personal goals and passions. It's a time for action and self-initiated projects. Trust your instincts and take the lead.

🕵 With Mercury's entrance into the enigmatic waters of Scorpio, your thinking gains depth and intensity. You're not satisfied with surface-level answers; you want to get to the heart of matters. You may find yourself drawn to uncovering truths and exploring the mysteries of life.

◐ The Full Moon, a celestial spotlight in the sky, shines a brilliant light on your path. It's a time of culmination and realization, where the intentions you set during the New Moon come to fruition. This moment brings clarity and a chance to reset your course.

OCTOBER WEEK TWO

As the Moon gracefully glides into Taurus, you're prompted to ground yourself in the earthly pleasures of life. Picture a cosmic embrace inviting you to revel in sensory delights, fostering a deeper connection with the tangible world. Feel the solid foundation beneath your feet, appreciating beauty and savoring the simple joys that contribute to your sense of inner peace.

The harmonious sextile between Venus, the enchantress of love, and expansive Jupiter paints your interactions with strokes of warmth and grace. This celestial alignment sets the stage for the blossoming of social connections, infusing your relationships with generosity and mutual understanding. It's a cosmic cue to share delightful moments with those who hold a special place in your heart, amplifying the joy that love brings.

Stepping into Gemini, the Moon invites you into a phase of heightened curiosity and intellectual exploration. Your mental landscape becomes a vibrant garden of ideas, with the desire for lively conversations and the pursuit of knowledge taking center stage. Engage in discussions and express your thoughts freely.

OCTOBER WEEK TWO

The direct motion of Pluto signals a decisive shift in cosmic currents, akin to a celestial phoenix rising from the ashes. This transformative period urges you to embrace profound inner growth and release any lingering shadows that hinder your evolution. It's a celestial call to welcome change and step into the light of personal rebirth.

The Moon's entrance into Leo adds a radiant and theatrical flair to the cosmic tapestry. This phase encourages you to bask in the spotlight.

Venus, in a harmonious trine with innovative Uranus, infuses a spark of excitement into your love life and creative endeavors. Embrace spontaneity and be open to unconventional expressions of affection, injecting an element of unpredictability into your experiences.

Venus's trine with Pluto deepens the emotional currents, fostering passion and intensity in your connections. This cosmic alliance invites transformative experiences in matters of the heart and creative pursuits, encouraging you to explore the profound depths of your emotions and desires.

OCTOBER WEEK THREE

◐ As the Moon gracefully enters Virgo, your focus shifts to the details and practicalities of daily life. This cosmic transition invites you to engage in acts of service and refine your routines. Embrace the meticulous energy of Virgo to enhance efficiency and create a harmonious environment that supports your well-being.

☉ The square between the Sun and expansive Jupiter adds a touch of cosmic tension, prompting you to examine the balance between confidence and humility. Navigate this energy by grounding your ambitions in practical steps, avoiding over-commitment, and seeking a realistic path toward your goals.

◐ Moving into Libra, the Moon encourages a shift toward harmony and balance in your emotional landscape. Cultivate grace in your interactions and strive for equilibrium in your relationships. Embrace the art of compromise and diplomacy, fostering connections that contribute to mutual understanding.

☿ Mercury's conjunction with assertive Mars injects your thoughts and communications with dynamic energy. It's a potent force for strategic thinking.

OCTOBER WEEK THREE

● The New Moon marks a cosmic reset, offering a blank canvas for new beginnings. It is ideal for setting intentions for personal growth, projects, or relationships. This lunar phase encourages you to plant seeds of intention that will gradually blossom in the coming weeks. Embrace the energy of initiation and innovation.

● As the Moon glides into Scorpio, emotions deepen, and a desire for authenticity arises. Explore the depths of your feelings, allowing vulnerability and emotional honesty to guide your interactions. This cosmic transit is a time for introspection and transformation.

In this week's cosmic journey, the Moon's transitions guide you through practicality, balance, assertiveness, and the potential for new beginnings. The Sun's square with Jupiter adds a layer of cosmic tension, urging thoughtful consideration of your ambitions. Mercury's conjunction with Mars empowers your thoughts and communication with assertive energy, while the New Moon signals a fresh start. The Moon's entry into Scorpio invites emotional depth and authenticity into your experiences.

OCTOBER WEEK FOUR

○ The Sun's ingress into Scorpio initiates a transformative period, inviting you to delve into the depths of your inner self. This Scorpio season encourages introspection, resilience, and the shedding of old layers. Embrace the opportunity for rebirth and regeneration as you navigate the mysterious waters of your emotions.

● The Sun's square with Pluto adds an intense cosmic flavor, urging you to confront power dynamics and hidden truths. Be prepared for a transformative encounter that challenges your understanding of personal power. This celestial alignment invites you to release what no longer serves you, paving the way for regeneration.

✦ Mercury's harmonious trine with Jupiter expands the realms of communication and knowledge. This alignment enhances intellectual pursuits, encouraging open-mindedness and the exploration of new ideas. Engage in meaningful conversations, and let the exchange of thoughts broaden your perspectives.

OCTOBER WEEK FOUR

📖 Mercury's trine with Neptune adds a dreamy and imaginative quality to your thoughts and communication. This cosmic dance enhances your intuition and creative expression. Embrace the flow of inspiration, allowing your mind to wander into the realms of fantasy and artistic exploration.

♐ Mercury's ingress into Sagittarius infuses your thinking with a sense of adventure and a thirst for knowledge. This cosmic shift encourages you to broaden your mental horizons, explore new philosophies, and embrace a more optimistic and expansive mindset.

☼ Mars' trine with Saturn brings a harmonious blend of energy and discipline. This cosmic alliance supports focused and strategic efforts, allowing you to make steady progress toward your goals. Use this cosmic momentum to overcome challenges with determination.

⚡ Mercury's opposition to Uranus introduces an element of unpredictability to your thoughts and communication. Be open to sudden insights and breakthroughs, but also remain flexible in the face of unexpected changes.

NOVEMBER WEEK ONE

🌙 The Moon charges into Aries, infusing the cosmic atmosphere with a burst of dynamic energy and a desire for bold initiatives. Embrace the spirited and adventurous vibes, and allow your emotions to lead you toward exciting new experiences and challenges.

💔 Venus squares Jupiter, creating a cosmic tension between the planet of love and beauty and the expansive energies of Jupiter. While this aspect may bring a sense of indulgence or extravagance, it's crucial to find balance. Be mindful of overindulgence, especially in matters of the heart and finances.

🚀 Mars forms a harmonious trine with Neptune, blending the assertive qualities of Mars with the dreamy and imaginative energies of Neptune. This cosmic alliance enhances your creativity, intuition, and spiritual pursuits. Use this energy to infuse passion into your dreams and projects.

🔥 Mars makes its fiery entrance into Sagittarius, setting the stage for dynamic and enthusiastic action. This transit encourages you to pursue goals with optimism and a willingness to explore uncharted territories.

NOVEMBER WEEK ONE

⚡ Mars opposed Uranus: This celestial alignment creates an atmosphere charged with electric and unpredictable energy. It's a time when sudden changes and unexpected events may occur, shaking up your usual routines and plans. There's a strong emphasis on breaking free from limitations and embracing liberation.

🌕 Full Moon: As the Full Moon illuminates the sky, it sheds light on your achievements and marks the culmination of your efforts. This transit is a time for reflection, where you can take stock of how far you've come, celebrate your successes, and acknowledge the hard work you've put in. It's also a period for letting go of anything that no longer aligns with your goals or serves your personal growth, allowing you to move forward with clarity and purpose.

🌋 Mars sextile Pluto: This powerful alignment brings a surge of determination and resilience. Your actions are fueled by a deep sense of purpose, making it easier to overcome obstacles and push through challenges. It's a time for harnessing your inner strength and using it to drive transformative changes in your endeavors, whether they be personal or professional.

NOVEMBER WEEK TWO

🌀 The cosmic dance intensifies as Uranus, the harbinger of change, steps into Taurus. This revolutionary shift promises a seismic transformation in the realms of stability and security, urging you to embrace adaptability and welcome groundbreaking ideas that may reshape the very foundations of your existence. This cosmic current invites you to open your heart to the unknown and trust in the process of metamorphosis.

💔 Venus locked in a complex tango with Pluto deepens the cosmic drama. This profound connection encourages you to delve into the intricate landscapes of your relationships. Like a cosmic alchemist, this aspect challenges you to confront hidden dynamics, transmuting challenges into opportunities for profound growth and a rebirth of the heart's desires.

🌙 The Moon's gentle transition into Cancer bathes the cosmic stage in emotional luminescence. This nurturing energy calls for prioritizing self-care and immersing yourself in the comforting embrace of loved ones. It's an invitation to honor your intuitive side, finding solace in the rhythmic dance of the lunar energies.

NOVEMBER WEEK TWO

Mercury, the cosmic messenger, embarks on its retrograde journey, initiating a period of introspection and review. During this cosmic pause, opportunities for revisiting old projects, relationships, and unresolved matters arise. Approach this time with mindfulness in communication, embrace the potential for delays, and relish the chance for profound self-reflection.

Jupiter, the expansive planet, takes a reflective pause as it turns retrograde. This cosmic realignment invites you to reassess personal beliefs, philosophies, and growth goals. Use this period for inner exploration, refining your understanding of your life's path, and making necessary adjustments for your continued evolution.

Mercury's dynamic conjunction with Mars injects the cosmic scene with heightened communication and mental agility. This dynamic pairing encourages assertive self-expression and empowers you to tackle tasks with precision. However, be mindful of potential conflicts that may arise from impulsive words, and channel this energy constructively.

NOVEMBER WEEK THREE

 Sun's trine with Saturn solidifies your cosmic support system. There's a harmonious dance between ambition and discipline, allowing you to lay solid foundations for your goals. This cosmic alliance suggests that patient and strategic efforts will be rewarded, bringing long-term stability and success.

 Mercury, the messenger planet, forms a dynamic sextile with transformative Pluto. Your communication style gains depth and power, allowing you to delve into profound conversations and uncover hidden truths. It's a time for meaningful exchanges that have an impact.

 Mercury's ingress into Scorpio deepens the cosmic currents, enhancing your ability to perceive beneath the surface. Your thoughts and communications take on a more intense and investigative tone. Dive into the mysteries, explore the nuances, and let truth guide you.

 A cosmic curveball arrives as Mercury opposes Uranus, introducing an element of unpredictability to your mental landscape. Sudden insights, innovative ideas, or unexpected communications may shake up your routine.

NOVEMBER WEEK THREE

● The New Moon marks the beginning of a new lunar cycle, urging you to set intentions and sow the seeds for future growth. It is a potent time for self-reflection and envisioning the path ahead. Embrace the energy of new beginnings and align your desires with the cosmic flow.

○ The Sun's conjunction with Mercury amplifies the cosmic spotlight on communication and self-expression. Your words carry weight, and your ideas have the potential to shine brightly. Use this time to articulate your thoughts with clarity and purpose.

♐ Mercury's transition into Sagittarius brings more adventurous and expansive energy to your mental landscape. It's a cosmic call to broaden your perspectives, engage in philosophical discussions, and explore the boundless realms of knowledge.

♅ Uranus's sextile with Neptune adds a dash of inspiration and innovation to your spiritual pursuits. This cosmic alliance encourages you to blend the realms of the tangible and the mystical, finding innovative ways to infuse your daily life with a sense of wonder.

NOVEMBER WEEK FOUR

🖊 Embark on a mental odyssey as Mercury trines Jupiter, expanding your intellectual horizons. Open your mind to grand ideas and explore broader concepts.

☽ Experience a transformative journey as the Sun sextiles Pluto, infusing your path with empowering energy. Tap into your inner strength and embrace positive changes. Overcome challenges with resilience and influence your circumstances positively. The cosmic support invites you to delve into personal growth and embrace the potential for transformation.

💙 Engage in heartfelt communication as Mercury conjuncts Venus. Charm and eloquence grace your words, enhancing your ability to express love and beauty. Let your expressions mirror the beauty that surrounds you, fostering harmony in your interactions.

🌈 Bask in the joyous atmosphere created by the harmonious trine between Venus and Jupiter. Abundance and pleasure intertwine in matters of love. Expand your capacity for love and enjoyment during this cosmic dance.

NOVEMBER WEEK FOUR

✦ Mercury turns direct, lifting the fog of retrograde energies. Communication flows smoothly, and delays or misunderstandings begin to resolve. Seize this time to make decisions, move plans forward, and express your thoughts with increased clarity.

⚡ Feel the tension and excitement as Venus opposes Uranus. Unexpected twists in love and relationships may arise. Embrace change and spontaneity, as unconventional elements add a spark of excitement to your romantic life or creative pursuits.

🔮 Experience a touch of magic and inspiration in relationships and artistic endeavors as Venus trines Neptune. Heightened sensitivity to beauty fosters a dreamy, romantic atmosphere. It's a perfect time for creative expression and spiritual growth.

🌿 Venus gracefully enters Sagittarius, infusing matters of the heart and pleasure with adventurous energy. Explore new avenues of love and enjoy life's joys with freedom and optimism. Embrace the spirit of adventure in relationships and creative pursuits as Venus dances through the expansive sign of Sagittarius.

DECEMBER WEEK ONE

☽ Embrace the luxurious energy as the Moon gracefully enters Taurus. This cosmic shift invites you to ground yourself in the earthly pleasures of life. Feel the comfort of stability and indulge in sensory delights. It's a time to savor the beauty that surrounds you and relish in the simple joys that touch your soul.

♥ Prepare for a cosmic dance as Venus forms a harmonious sextile with Pluto. Love and transformation intertwine in a sultry embrace. Your relationships take on a magnetic allure, drawing you into the depths of connection and passion. Embrace the transformative power of love, and let its magic weave through the fabric of your heart.

☽ The Moon pirouettes into Gemini, ushering in a breeze of intellectual curiosity. Your mind dances with versatility and a thirst for knowledge. Embrace the joy of learning and engage in stimulating conversations that tickle your intellect. It's a time of mental agility and the delightful exploration of diverse ideas.

DECEMBER WEEK ONE

Ah, the cosmic spectacle of a Full Moon graces the night sky. The lunar glow illuminates your emotions, casting a radiant light on the tapestry of your inner world. Release what no longer serves you and bask in the fullness of your emotional truth. The universe whispers its secrets, and you stand bathed in the lunar glow of revelation.

The Moon steps into nurturing Cancer, wrapping you in a cosmic embrace of emotional sensitivity. Feelings swell and flow like the gentle tide. Create a sanctuary for your heart, and let the waves of emotion guide you to a place of introspection and self-care. Your intuition becomes a guiding light in this tender lunar transition.

Mercury forms a harmonious trine with Neptune, casting a dreamy veil over your thoughts and communications. Your words become poetry, and your mind drifts into the realms of imagination. It's a time to express your dreams and listen to the subtle whispers of the universe. Let the cosmic current carry you into the waters of inspiration.

DECEMBER WEEK TWO

◐ Mars squares off against Saturn, creating a celestial clash that calls for a delicate dance between assertion and restraint. This cosmic tension demands a strategic and patient approach to your ambitions. Consider this a stellar training ground where the disciplined warrior within you can emerge.

☾ The Moon gracefully pirouettes into meticulous Virgo, casting a spotlight on the details of your emotions. It's a prime opportunity to declutter your mental space and infuse practicality into your inner world. Embrace a systematic approach to your feelings, finding beauty in the precision of emotional organization.

◉ Neptune, the Dreamweaver, resumes direct motion, lifting the cosmic fog that shrouded your dreams. With newfound clarity, your inspirations take shape, beckoning you to trust your intuitive compass. The ethereal realms are now open for exploration, and your connection to the mystical deepens.

DECEMBER WEEK TWO

♆ Mercury's trine with Neptune adds a touch of enchantment to your communications. Express your ideas with creativity and compassion, and watch as your words weave a tapestry of understanding. It's a time when your communication transcends the mundane and touches the soul.

♐ Mercury, the celestial messenger, dons the adventurous attire of Sagittarius. Your thoughts now embark on a journey of exploration and expansion. Open your mind to the vast landscapes of knowledge, and let your intellectual curiosity soar.

♎ The Moon gracefully waltzes into Libra, bringing a sense of equilibrium to your emotional realm. Seek harmony in your relationships, and appreciate the beauty that arises when balance is found.

♇ Mercury's harmonious sextile with Pluto intensifies your communications. Dive into deep, transformative conversations, and let the power of your words bring about positive change. Your thoughts carry an extra punch now, capable of reshaping the very fabric of your reality.

DECEMBER WEEK THREE

♐ As Mars, the cosmic warrior, strides into disciplined Capricorn, the battleground shifts to matters of ambition and achievement. Your drive intensifies, and strategic actions pave the way for substantial progress. Channel this energy into your pursuits, scaling the peaks of your aspirations.

◯ A cosmic challenge unfolds as the Sun squares off against stern Saturn. This celestial standoff urges you to confront obstacles with resilience and patience. Consider it a cosmic reality check, prompting you to fortify your foundations before reaching for the stars.

◐ The Moon dons the cloak of adventurous Sagittarius, inspiring a sense of wanderlust and exploration. Embrace the spirit of curiosity, and let your emotions roam freely across the vast landscapes of possibility.

● The New Moon graces the celestial canvas, signaling a potent moment for new beginnings. Plant the seeds of your intentions, and watch them sprout into manifestations in the lunar cycle ahead. Set your aspirations alight with the flame of fresh starts.

DECEMBER WEEK THREE

☾ The Sun squares off against dreamy Neptune, creating a dance between reality and illusion. Exercise caution in matters requiring clarity and discernment. Ensure that your dreams are grounded in practicality to avoid potential pitfalls.

💔 Venus engages in a cosmic tango with Saturn, prompting a reassessment of your relationships and values. While challenges may arise, they offer opportunities for growth and strengthening the foundations of your connections.

☉ The December Solstice marks a turning point, heralding the official beginning of winter (or summer in the southern hemisphere). It's a celestial reminder of the cyclical nature of life and an invitation to align with the rhythms of the cosmos.

♑ The Sun's entrance into Capricorn, the sign of ambition and discipline, aligns with the energy of the season. It's a time for setting intentions, focusing on long-term goals, and drawing upon the determination needed to navigate the path ahead.

DECEMBER WEEK FOUR

💜 With Venus entering a celestial dance with Neptune, a captivating yet intricate energy surrounds matters of the heart. The lines between reality and illusion may blur, emphasizing the importance of careful discernment in your approach to relationships. Guard against excessive idealization of situations or individuals, and strive for clarity in your emotional connections.

⭐ Venus gracefully moves into the structured realm of Capricorn, infusing a sense of order and responsibility into your expressions of love and appreciation for beauty. During this phase, practical considerations may play a significant role in your romantic pursuits, encouraging you to establish strong foundations. Thoughtful gestures of love could be incredibly impactful during this period.

🌙 The Moon glides into the dreamy waters of Pisces, inviting you to explore the poetic landscapes of emotion and intuition. This celestial alignment enhances your sensitivity and compassion, creating an ideal moment for artistic endeavors, meditation, or introspective journeys to connect with your inner self.

DECEMBER WEEK FOUR

♈ Step into a cosmic shift as the Moon confidently strides into Aries, unleashing a surge of initiative and a burning desire for action. Let this dynamic force propel you forward, urging you to tackle challenges head-on.

♣ Embark on a celestial journey as the Moon gracefully transitions into the grounded realms of Taurus. Immerse yourself in the sensory pleasures of the material world, finding tranquility and solace in the stability of your immediate surroundings. Revel in the tangible comforts that bring joy to your senses.

☐ Witness the celestial clash between Mercury and Saturn, creating a cosmic tension that challenges the balance between communication and structure. Navigate this celestial tussle with careful and deliberate expression, being attuned to potential obstacles in conveying your ideas. Embrace patience and diligence in your communication, using this period to refine and shape your thoughts.

♊ Behold the Moon's elegant pirouette into the inquisitive realms of Gemini, igniting intellectual curiosity and enhancing your communication skills.

NOTES

NOTES

NOTES

Astrology, Tarot & Horoscope Books.

Mystic Cat

www.ingramcontent.com/pod-product-compliance
Lightning Source LLC
LaVergne TN
LVHW051844080426
835512LV00018B/3061